CAREERS IN
FOREIGN LANGUAGES

TEACHERS, TRANSLATORS, INTERPRETERS

ACHIEVING FLUENCY IN A FOREIGN language can lead to a career as a teacher or translator, both of which offer many opportunities to travel while you help others to accomplish their goals. Teachers help other people to learn foreign languages. Translators concentrate on translating written texts into another language. Interpreters translate spoken language.

You are exploring this career at a very good time. It has become common to note that the world is shrinking, and that international relations are more important than ever before. Never before in human history have so many people been involved in professions that require fluency in multiple languages. Demand for teachers and translators has never been higher.

WHAT YOU CAN DO NOW

YOU CAN GET STARTED ON YOUR career in foreign languages right now. Take as many language classes as you can in high school. Maybe English is already your second language or you speak a language other than English with your family. Even native speakers need training in the finer points of grammar. Spanish is taught just about everywhere, and French and German are also very common. Languages once thought to be of little use to Americans, like Chinese and Arabic, are now offered in some high schools. Pursue at least two, even if you plan to specialize in only one. You will spend even more time working the linguistic parts of your brain and you might even discover that learning two new languages is not as hard as you thought.

Many high schools offer foreign exchange programs or summer study abroad programs. This experience guarantees that you will achieve some fluency in the language spoken where you do your exchange. You will have to speak a target language pretty well to qualify for a foreign exchange program, because most such programs put visiting students directly into classes alongside local students. After a year of using French every day you will almost certainly be fluent. Foreign exchange programs typically require students to commit to spending an entire year living abroad with a host family. There is no better way to learn a language than to be immersed in it.

The internet has placed most of the world's publications within easy reach. Want to brush up your Russian? Check out www.pravda.ru. French? www.france24.com/fr. For Spanish, go to this website www.cronica.com.mx. The British Broadcasting Corporation publishes news in 28 different languages at www.bbc.co.uk. Make it a point to read some news in another language every day.

HISTORY OF THE CAREER

THE FIRST HUMANS TO BAND together into small, nomadic groups hundreds of thousands of years ago devised languages to communicate with others. When they needed to describe something, they invented a word for it. When different tribes bumped into each other during their travels, there was often confusion, if not violence, because members of each tribe had no idea what others were trying to say. If your tribe was perceived as a threat you probably would not have time to learn the other tribe's language while dodging their rocks and spears.

This began to change about 10,000 years ago when the advent of agriculture allowed wandering bands of humans to settle down in one place indefinitely. Freed from the need to follow herds of game in order to eat, people could put down roots anywhere they could grow crops. Populations boomed in these new settlements, naturally absorbing the languages of earlier tribes and creating new languages spoken by many more people.

There used to be many more languages than there are now. Nobody knows the exact number, but until well into the 1500s even the countries of Europe were splintered into dozens of regional dialects that could not be understood a few counties away from their home base. From its role as the official language of the Roman Empire, Latin tied together the Western world for thousands of years. Aristocrats, religious leaders, and commercial traders all used Latin to communicate with each other. Latin was not the language of the common people, however. In fact, colloquial languages used by regular people were known as "vulgate," which shares a Latin root with the modern word "vulgar." The common people of France, for example, spoke versions of French that differed from one place to another. The advent of the printing press in the 1440s began to standardize languages through a process known as "print capitalism." The owners of printing presses wanted to sell more books, so they standardized languages so they could be read by more people. A typesetter at a print shop selling books within two counties with similar dialects would make subtle changes to a text so that it could be understood by people fluent in either dialect. The process was repeated until one common language was used across an entire country.

Even today there are about 7,000 languages still used around the world. Some of these are used by very few people, like tribal languages still spoken in pockets of Africa, Asia, the Amazon Basin in South America, and on Indian reservations in the United States. The United Nations reaches most of the world's people by translating everything it does into only six languages: Arabic, Chinese, English, French, Russian, and Spanish. The entire Western Hemisphere uses only four official languages: English, French, Portuguese, and Spanish.

Language education began in earnest in the 19th century and was based on rote translation. Students were taught grammar and vocabulary at a slow but steady pace and given assignments to translate texts from one language into another. Students were also expected to memorize charts of verb conjugations and do endless drills that were meant to enforce learning by repetition.

Such methods are still employed in language teaching today, especially in high schools. Grammar translation is common, as is the audio-lingual method of repeating phrases until they come naturally. Situational teaching concentrates on placing students into common situations and giving them the necessary vocabulary to figure out what to say, such as greetings or asking for directions. Interactive methods are by far the most popular today. Interactive methods attempt to replicate the conditions under which people learn their native languages. Children learn languages in part by being taught by their parents and other people around them, and also simply by listening to others. Nobody ever taught you how to conjugate a verb in your native language.

The ultimate form of language learning is total immersion. Students often spend a summer or semester studying abroad just to immerse themselves in their target language. The necessity of being understood quickly overcomes fears of sounding stupid. The problem with immersion is that it is expensive and difficult to arrange. Given the opportunity, who wouldn't want to spend a summer in Paris soaking up French? Seize these opportunities while you are young and can arrange the financing for it.

The internet allows more people than ever before to enjoy at least some of the advantages of total immersion. It is easy to take one-on-one lessons from a native speaker via online video, for example. Rosetta Stone software uses the internet to link together language learners from around the globe so they can chat with each other and polish their skills. As a foreign language professional you will be able to take advantage of these opportunities both as a learner and as a teacher, translator or interpreter.

WHERE YOU WILL WORK

MANY INDUSTRIES ARE CONCENTRATED in a few places. Careers in foreign languages are dispersed around the world. Few careers offer as wide a variety of places to live. Almost every career in foreign languages demands some time spent outside the United States. Many professionals in this field start out as immigrants or the children of immigrants and have built-in connections to other countries and cultures. People who choose to learn foreign languages often do so out of a desire to broaden their horizons and learn more about the world. If you choose to pursue this career you will probably be required to spend time abroad, and you will want to.

There is a world of difference between translating French in an office building in Paris and serving as an interpreter for a nongovernmental organization operating in Cameroon, a French-speaking country in West Africa. Some linguists prefer the sophistication of international commerce and diplomacy, while others prefer an adventure off the beaten path. Your skills will open many doors wherever you go.

Living abroad is a life-changing experience. The world is a very large, very diverse place with many different customs and attitudes. A few years in somebody else's world will make you see your own through very different eyes. Most of the world's people are more concerned about basic necessities like clean drinking water than they are about the latest smartphone.

Translation, interpretation and teaching jobs are available all over the United States. There are especially large concentrations at universities and in major cities. Universities often have foreign language and international studies programs that require many linguists, while big cities are home to most of the international business community.

DESCRIPTION OF WORK DUTIES

Foreign Language Teachers

Foreign language teachers are the essential professionals in foreign languages. Translators, interpreters and other teachers would not be able to enter their careers without first spending time under the tutelage of a foreign-language teacher. Their skills are the keys to achieving everything else.

There are many ways to become a foreign language teacher. Your first thought may be teachers working in elementary or high schools. These careerists are usually the first contact most people have with foreign language learning. Teachers in public school districts are usually responsible for teaching four or five classes per day, five days per week. High school teachers typically teach several levels of language simultaneously. That is, they may teach two sections of first-year language and one section each of second-, third-, and fourth-year language in the same day. This requires keeping track of many students and grading hundreds of papers and tests. It is also an excellent way to maintain your own language skills. Teachers at the elementary and junior-high levels usually have only two levels to teach.

Most public school districts offer a wide array of benefits including paid sick leave and vacation time, a guaranteed pension after a set period of service – usually about 30 years –

and health insurance coverage. Public school districts also offer the three biggest benefits that come with teaching careers: "June, July and August." Many teachers, and especially foreign language teachers, take advantage of the summer months to travel and have an opportunity to use their foreign language skills while soaking up the culture in another country.

To get into public school teaching, careerists typically need to earn a bachelor's degree and a teaching credential for the state they want to work in. Earning a teaching credential usually requires that students spend a semester as a student teacher working alongside a veteran teacher in a real-world environment. Many careerists go on to earn master's degrees, often on a part-time basis while they are working in the classroom. They do so because they want to learn more about their subject, and also because most school districts pay teachers more money for earning additional degrees.

The formula is very much the same for teachers in private schools, although expectations may be different. Some parochial schools may expect teachers to do more with less, while some secular private schools may have higher budgets and offer extra advantages, like language learning labs and field trips to restaurants serving indigenous foods.

Many foreign language teachers do not work in traditional schools. They may work as full-time teachers for businesses or government agencies whose employees need language training in order to do their jobs. They may also work for foreign language schools like ALTA or Berlitz that specialize in teaching languages mostly to adults. These careerists can have many different work arrangements. Some are freelancers who get paid by the hour or class. The internet would make it possible for a freelancer in Washington State to teach a student in Virginia as a freelancer for a foreign language school based in Georgia.

TESOL Teachers

Teachers of English to speakers of other languages (TESOL) are foreign language teachers. You may not have considered this possibility because, for you, English is not a foreign language. It will be to your students, however. Many American college students earn TESOL certificates to enable them to work in English language schools all over the world. There are thousands to choose from, and most governments are happy to provide work visas to English teachers to enable them to work legally. Many English speakers have financed trips around the world by teaching English as they go, stopping for a few months in one country and maybe a year in another.

Becoming a TESOL teacher has two main benefits. First, it will teach you about language learning in general. You will learn by putting yourself in the teacher's shoes even if you have no desire to become a teacher for your entire career. Second, spending some time as a TESOL teacher is a great way to improve fluency in your target language. If your target language is Portuguese, for example, a year spent working at a TESOL school in Brazil will give you daily opportunities to improve your Portuguese and will not cost you anything because you will have a paying job while you are there. Spending a year abroad with a salary is obviously preferable to spending that year living solely on your savings.

The easiest way to earn a TESOL certificate is to work it into your studies while in college or immediately thereafter. Your school may offer a TESOL program through its extension campus or graduate school. Armed with a bachelor's degree and a TESOL certificate you can email your résumé to TESOL schools in countries all around the world. While fluency in the local language is generally not a requirement for TESOL jobs, it certainly can help. Relatively few people pursue careers in TESOL for the long run, but many do it for a few years early in their careers to take advantage of this unparalleled opportunity. Some come back to it later in life after they have retired from their full-time careers, just to have a little fun and adventure.

Translators

Translators translate written documents into languages other than the one they were written in. This process of conversion is about much more than simply replacing each word with its equivalent in another language. The finished translated document must read like it had been written in the new language in the first place.

Translators must achieve perfect fluency in their target language in order to be effective. They may also use computer applications and language dictionaries in order to maintain consistency and solve thorny problems. Most translation is a matter of adapting simple grammar rules to convert sentences from one language into another. Words and tenses often need to be shifted around in order to convey the same meaning from one language to the other – but there is more to it than that. Successful translators also have to get to know their target language inside out. That means learning the idiomatic phrases and colloquialisms used by regular people in everyday speech. In English, for example, we often use phrases like "sour grapes" or "white elephant" to stand in for much larger ideas. In this case, speakers of American colloquial English know that "sour grapes" has nothing to do with fruit but instead describes a feeling of resentment based on past slights that may or may not be legitimate. Likewise, a "white elephant" is something that has outlived its usefulness but is large and hard to ignore or get rid of, like an abandoned building. Speakers of colloquial French use the phrase "se crasser la tete" when they want to imply that somebody is thinking very hard about something. Literally translated, the phrase means "to break one's head." A translator working in French needs to know that remarks about breaking heads probably do not mean anything about actually doing that unless they are found in a police report describing a terrible accident. The only way to gain this level of comprehension in a foreign language is to use it every day, preferably with native speakers.

Many translators are generalists able to work in just about any arena. Some industries require specialized expertise, however. Among these are medicine, law, and literature. In the case of medicine and law, an error in translation could have dire consequences. For literature, translators have to have enough facility with the language to be able to preserve the original author's style and intent when converting the author's words into a new language.

Interpreters

Interpreters translate speech as it is being spoken. Unlike translators, interpreters cannot reach for the dictionary or type a troublesome phrase into a computer when they need a little help. They have to make the decision immediately.

Interpretation falls into three broad categories: simultaneous, consecutive, and whispered. Simultaneous interpretation takes place in conjunction with the original speech. This is usually done with the aid of electronic systems that allow listeners to hear spoken words in their own languages. The most famous use of simultaneous interpretation is at the United Nations headquarters in New York, where an army of interpreters make sure that all delegates sitting in the General Assembly can understand every word spoken by whomever is at the podium. Watch a video of a UN meeting and you will see that most delegates are wearing headphones. Look above the assembly floor and you will notice a long row of windows. Behind those windows are interpreters watching the speeches and interpreting what is said into whatever languages the delegates need to hear. They do this in real time, usually only a few seconds behind the original speaker.

Consecutive interpretation takes place after the original words have been spoken. A speaker says a sentence or two and then waits while an interpreter converts the words into another language. Whispered interpretation is a hybrid of simultaneous and consecutive interpretation, where an interpreter whispers the converted language into the ear of the person for whom he/she is working. Whispered is often favored by diplomats and business executives who need communication to be as seamless as possible.

STORIES OF FOREIGN LANGUAGE PROFESSIONALS

I Am a High School French Teacher

"I always knew that I wanted to be a teacher. I didn't always know that I wanted to teach a foreign language, however. I discovered that during a summer trip to France while I was in high school. I took French in high school because I needed to take at least two years of a foreign language and French sounded cool. I enjoyed it, and it showed in my good grades. I decided to take four years of French in high school.

During the summer between my junior and senior years some of my fellow students and I went on a two-week trip to France organized by my school. It was our French teacher, a couple of parental chaperones and 15 students. We went to Paris, toured the wine country, saw the beaches at Normandy, and ate lots of cheese and baguettes. It was the first time I had been outside of the United States. I realized that there is a very large world out there that isn't like America at all, but has a whole lot to offer. That's when I decided to become a French teacher.

In college I double-majored in French and education, which is common for teachers. You major in both teaching and the subject you want to teach. During college I spent a year studying abroad in Paris, which was an amazing experience. Needing to use a language all day, every day is without question the best way to learn a second language and keep it forever. I also completed an internship in my senior year working as a translator and interpreter for a local company that did business in Quebec, the French-speaking part of Canada. Then there was student teaching in order to earn a teaching credential in my state.

I usually teach four classes per day, five days a week. I teach two sections of first-year French, which is always the most in-demand, and one section each of second-year and third-year. I am one of two French teachers at my school, so we change our schedules every year for variety.

I enjoy teaching the first-year students the most. That's when they are just beginning to understand the concept of learning a foreign language. Usually I can tell who will stick with it and who won't after a few months. Not everybody is wired to learn languages. Some kids remember everything and seem to have an intuitive sense of what is right and what is wrong, linguistically speaking. Others get through with rote memorization.

I love my job because it lets me focus on something I truly love and get paid for it. I am working on a master's degree in French literature, which will result in a sizable raise in my salary. My proudest moment came a few years ago when it was my turn to lead the annual summer trip to France. Everything had come full circle."

I Am a Translator and Interpreter for a Nongovernmental Organization

"I am whatever the situation needs me to be – translator, interpreter, or teacher. I am employed by a nongovernmental organization working mostly in the Lusophone countries of Africa.

What makes a country "Lusophone?" The fact that its people speak Portuguese. Just like an Anglophone country is English speaking and a Francophone country is French speaking, a

Lusophone country is Portuguese speaking. Portugal administered an enormous empire from the early 1400s to 2002, when it granted independence to East Timor (its last remaining colony). More than 250 million people today speak Portuguese as their first language, making it one of the most widely-spoken languages in the world. It is closely related to Spanish, and Spanish and Portuguese speakers can often understand each other with a little effort.

I chose to study Portuguese because I wanted to see the world and do something a little different. I studied in Lisbon while I was in college, and I returned shortly after graduation to work as a TESOL teacher and continue to polish my skills in Portuguese. It was a smart move for many reasons. During my years in Portugal, I was introduced to the Lusophone African diaspora. Many Lusophone Africans live in Portugal. Some come to get a good education at a Portuguese university, some come for business reasons, and some just come to build better lives for themselves in Europe.

I made many friends within the Africa community, and became interested in the cultures and countries that they came from. There are six Portuguese speaking countries in Africa, all of which are poor and in need of various kinds of assistance. They are Angola, Cape Verde, Guinea-Bissau, Mozambique, and Sao Tome and Principe. Portuguese is also one of three official languages in Equatorial Guinea, where most residents speak Spanish as their first language.

A few years ago I started working for a nongovernmental organization, or NGO, based in the United States that helps to bring clean water to remote villages in Africa. NGOs are important players in the world of international development because they can often ignore the political pressures that sometimes make it difficult for governments to provide assistance to people who need it.

My job is to be the linguist-on-the-spot. I interpret conversations between our staffers and locals, I translate documents like instruction manuals and legal papers, and I spend a little time each day teaching Portuguese to our American personnel and English to our Lusophone partners. I also assist with the grunt work of laying pipe and generally getting the odd jobs done, although I was hired for my linguistic skills.

I love my career because it has enabled me to go places and do things that I could never have imagined without a second language. I would urge anybody considering this career to think outside the box when it comes time to find a job. Anybody can translate documents in an office in the United States. I probably will someday, when I'm a little older and the idea of sleeping in a tent for months at a time is no longer so appealing. Until that day comes, I want to use my skills to have adventures most people will never get to have. That's what gets me excited about my career."

I Am a TESOL Teacher

"I majored in English, which isn't exactly a foreign language for an American. Like many English majors, I wasn't sure what I wanted to do after graduation but I knew that it had to be exciting. A degree in English doesn't necessarily put you on any particular path, so I figured I would sort it out as I went along.

On a lark, I decided to spend a semester studying abroad in Italy. I like the food and the art museums. Italian language classes were part of the curriculum, of course, along with history, music, and art. I liked it so much I stayed for an entire academic year.

As much as I enjoyed the culture of Italy, my biggest discovery was the fact there are TESOL schools everywhere. Like most Europeans, Italians want to learn English. It is the world's first choice for commerce, science and media. It is also the easiest way for people who don't speak each other's native language to communicate, because almost everybody speaks a little English.

After graduation I immediately earned a TESOL certificate. Armed with the certificate and a bachelor's degree in English I sent résumés to a handful of TESOL schools in Italy. I was offered a job fairly quickly. The Italian government, like many governments, makes it easy for properly credentialed careerists to get work visas to teach English. The visa is for one year, requires sponsorship by an employer, and is easily renewed at the end of the year, if you want to stay.

So I spent two years in Italy working full time as a TESOL teacher. I made many friends and polished up my Italian simply by virtue of living in Italy. I also made many friends in the TESOL community, which is a jackpot of connections and information about TESOL opportunities. After my time in Italy, I went to Portugal to work at a TESOL school affiliated with the one I worked at in Italy. I never set out to learn Portuguese, but what the heck. It's a Romance language, and very similar to Italian, so it didn't take long to pick it up.

After two years in Portugal I have so many options my biggest problem is choosing among them. Should I get an MBA and go into international business? Go back to the United States and start a career as a foreign-language teacher in Italian or Portuguese? Or maybe pick a new country and a new TESOL opportunity? If too many choices is my biggest problem, life is pretty good."

I Am a Freelance Arabic Linguist

"Translators, interpreters and teachers of Romance languages like Spanish and French are pretty common. There's no doubt that the market is filled with capable linguists in Western languages. That's why I pursued fluency in Arabic. Now, I get to pick and choose my jobs.

I started my career in the United States military. I wasn't sure what I wanted to do, so I took the placement test for linguists. It's kind of fun. They give you a made-up language and test your ability to figure it out. You are eligible for training in certain languages depending upon your score. A lower passing score makes you eligible for a familiar Western language like French or German. Higher scores can set you up for training in languages like Arabic and Chinese. I did really well on the test and chose Arabic as my language.

I've never been able to decide if military language training is easy or hard. For most people, learning a language is difficult because it's something you have to squeeze into your spare time. The military doesn't have that problem. Languages are taught at the Defense Language Institute in Monterey, California. Classes are from 8 a.m. to 5 p.m., Monday through Friday. Students are required to use their target language all day, every day. Even at lunch or during bathroom breaks. Romance language programs take six months. Most other languages take a year.

I put my skills to use immediately after graduation by serving on a civil affairs team in the Middle East. Our job was to go out into the communities recently scarred by combat operations and make friends with the local people. We listened to their concerns and offered help where we could. Those people were not our enemies. Most of the regular people in a combat zone are just that – regular people. We did everything we could to rebuild infrastructure, schools, and even entire neighborhoods. Each civil affairs team includes at least one person who speaks the local language. I won't kid you. Getting so up-close-and-personal with the after effects of war wasn't exactly fun but I took pride in tackling a difficult job and doing it well.

After finishing my five year hitch I went on to cash in my GI Bill on a bachelor's degree in Arabic and Middle Eastern studies. I started freelancing right away, translating Arabic documents into English and vice-versa. I got freelance jobs at my university and through local translation companies that hire people with skills like mine.

I've been a freelance Arabic linguist ever since. I worked on contracts for the Departments of Defense and State, worked for some companies doing business in the Middle East, done a fair bit of traveling, and generally enjoyed myself. In the world of foreign language careers, Arabic skills pay quite well. That first year of language school was hard, but it was worth every minute."

PERSONAL QUALIFICATIONS

YOU MUST HAVE AN INNATE ABILITY for learning languages. Some people are better at learning languages than others. It is a knack, just like some people can sit down at a piano and pick out a tune by ear. Can you pick up basic phrases easily? How about developing a feel for languages that allows you to figure out what new words mean just by clues like their place in the sentence and their similarity to other words you already know? Being a translator or interpreter is about much more than simply changing words into different languages. Translators need to understand the subtleties of their languages. Every little nuance needs to be clear. When there is not a simple translation, you have to be able to devise one based on literal definitions, shades of meaning, and commonly understood connotations.

Learning language to this degree requires a keen ear for cultural quirks and subtleties. Many phrases are loaded with cultural significance that must be understood in order to be translated properly. The French, for example, use the phrase "le grandeur" to describe political actions taken to preserve the grandeur of France, like maintaining an independent nuclear arsenal or pouring billions of euros into restoring the opulent palace of Versailles. French people know what "le grandeur" means. A translator will need to know that and many other slang expressions. These quirks can be found in all languages. In British

English, to "knock someone up" means to drop by their home and knock on the door.

The only way to learn these nuances and then interpret them for others is to have exceptional interpersonal skills. If you are shy and withdrawn, you will be unlikely to grasp the little linguistic quirks used by real people in real speech – which is not like formal speech learned in class or from books. You need to enjoy talking to people and listening closely to what they have to say.

ATTRACTIVE FEATURES

A CAREER IN FOREIGN LANGUAGES can be glamorous and exciting. Fluency in more than one language is a key that will unlock many doors. You may have your long-term sights set on a reliable, predictable career as a high-school language teacher or an in-house translator and interpreter for a multinational company. Such careers offer steady paychecks, good benefits, respect from your friends and family, and the satisfaction of doing something you enjoy. In the short term, your skills will allow you to indulge in more exciting opportunities. You could teach TESOL in a foreign country, do a hitch in the Peace Corps or the military, work as a freelance interpreter for a nongovernmental organization doing vital work, or even just strap on a backpack and hit the road for a year or two and soak up a new culture. You may even decide that you want to live this exciting life for the long term and get into something you had never considered before, like international business or diplomacy.

If you want to gain a deeper understanding of the world, a career in foreign languages is an excellent way to do it. Most of the world's people do not live like Americans. They do not think like Americans, hold similar values, or lead similar lives. All this can be confusing to people who do not take the time to understand and appreciate other cultures. Studying a foreign language guarantees that you will learn about at least one culture other than your own, and probably several. French, Arabic, and Spanish are spoken all around the world. Devoting a few years to learning to speak French, for example, does not mean that you will only learn about French culture. With a little effort you can also learn about several North and West African cultures, some Middle Eastern cultures and a few Polynesian cultures, and you can do it in their language. Studying a foreign language is one of the best ways to understand what happens behind the headlines.

Whether you become a teacher, translator, interpreter or some combination of all three, you will always be helping other people to achieve something that is important to them. Teachers help people to learn foreign languages in order to achieve their own goals. Translators and interpreters enable people to conduct business without learning a foreign language on their own. There is a great deal of satisfaction in helping others to reach their goals.

UNATTRACTIVE ASPECTS

NOBODY GETS RICH IN FOREIGN languages unless you use it as a stepping-stone to something else. Teachers, translators and interpreters can live comfortable, secure, middle-class lives. Their skills will always be in demand and they will enjoy moderate earnings. That is why many careerists who start out pursuing foreign languages eventually get into something else, like international business or diplomacy. A few years spent working for high-powered, globetrotting business executives as a reliable translator may convince you that you need to earn an MBA (Master of Business Administration degree) and get in the game yourself. Similarly, you may be discouraged always standing on the sidelines as an interpreter at international conferences or other diplomatic functions. Why not pursue a degree in international relations and become part of the conversation, rather than simply the person who helps the conversation along?

Foreign language professionals are usually small cogs in big machines. Your skills may make it possible for two business titans to negotiate a deal, for example, but when it is all done you will not be among the people shaking hands and patting themselves on the back for a job well done. You will be among the throngs of helpers whose contributions are taken for granted. There is not really anything wrong with this. You show up, do your best, collect your paycheck and do it again. But those high level negotiations you help to make happen will never be about you. The only way to get past this reality is to build your own business. The kind of business where you are the person hiring the freelancers and sending them out to the clients who need them.

Linguists often burn out after a decade or two. As interesting as it can be, translation and interpretation can also become repetitive and dull. Teacher burnout is a common phenomenon. Are there ways to avoid burnout? Earn a new credential from time to time. Have a new experience that will enhance your career. Learn a new skill and figure out how to work it into your daily routine.

EDUCATION AND TRAINING

EVEN IF YOU WERE LUCKY ENOUGH TO GROW up speaking more than one language, there is still much you will have to learn before you can put your linguistic skills to use professionally. You should plan to go to college and earn a bachelor's degree. You may even want to earn a graduate degree later in your career.

Majoring in your target language is obviously your best choice in college. Many careerists with an eye on a foreign-language career double major in two different languages, or at least major in one language and minor in another. Some universities offer concentrations in teaching or in translation and interpretation within their foreign language majors. College is the last time in your life that you will be able to indulge yourself in learning languages, all day, every day, with all the teachers and learning resources you could ever want. Learning a language later in life can be much more difficult. As we get older it becomes harder to learn new languages.

The languages that you will want to study depend upon what you want to do. Do you dream of traveling to or working in a particular part of the world? If so, naturally target a language or two that will get you there. Do you want to get ahead in a particular business or profession? Arabic is useful in the oil business. If you can speak Chinese, Arabic, Russian or Pashtu, the military will definitely want to sign you up. Common European languages like French and German are always in demand, and Portuguese and Italian have many uses. Targeting an uncommon language like Uzbek, will put you at the head of the line for opportunities in Uzbekistan, but there are limited opportunities in Uzbekistan. A common language like French offers more opportunities but also more competition. Learning a language is first and foremost a labor of love, and you should pursue languages that interest you.

You should also consider studying a language in conjunction with another field, like education, international studies, or business administration. There is no denying that having a complimentary skill set will go a long way toward enhancing your job opportunities. Take a look at the requirements for a major or minor in a complementary subject.

There are two specific opportunities you should not pass up

while you are in college. First, you must study abroad. Most colleges and universities offer study abroad programs. Pick one that will force you to use your target language. Go for at least a semester, and preferably a full year, in order to completely immerse yourself in your new language. Never again will it be so easy to take off to a foreign country for a year and learn all about a new language and culture. If you are learning two languages, study abroad twice. Some colleges require students to spend at least one semester abroad in order to graduate.

The other thing you should do is complete an internship. Simply stated, an internship is a full-time job that takes the place of classes for a summer or semester. Most internships are paid and many come with special seminars and other opportunities not generally offered to regular employees. In your case, an internship could be abroad, working for a foreign company where you can use your new language, or it could be at home in a related field like foreign language teaching. An internship will give you valuable professional experience to put on your résumé. It is very common for former interns to find their first job after college with the company where they did their internship.

There are other ways to learn languages. The United States military trains thousands of language experts every year to assist in dealings with foreign militaries and to serve in fields like intelligence and cryptography. If you already know another language, that is great. If not, the military will administer a test that determines how well you can figure out a made-up language. If you do well, it means you have a natural aptitude for languages and can be taught whatever language the military needs. That could be something not offered in any civilian school. About the only language the military does not need is Spanish, and that is only because it already recruits plenty of Spanish speakers. Many linguists get their start in the military. Even if you do not make the military a lifetime career, one five-year hitch can get you advanced language training, incredible experiences you cannot have anywhere else, and eligibility for the GI Bill, which will pay for a college degree after you get out.

Another favored way to learn foreign languages is to teach English to speakers of other languages, or TESOL (often also known as ESL, for "English as a second language"). Many linguists earn TESOL teaching certificates in conjunction with their language studies because a certificate enables them to get jobs teaching English abroad. Working at an English language school in Tokyo is a great way to work on your Japanese. TESOL schools can be found all over the world and are a popular option for adventurous travelers who want to be able to make some money while they see the world. Learning how to teach other people your native language is also a great way to learn more about language learning in general.

Will you need to go to graduate school? That depends entirely upon your career path. Most linguists and translators do not need advanced degrees. Teachers, however, may very well benefit from advanced degrees in their target languages.

EARNINGS

KEEP YOUR SKILLS IN SHAPE AND YOU can expect to earn a decent living almost anywhere. This goes for both salaried positions and freelance opportunities.

Full-time translators and interpreters can expect to earn about $45,000 to $55,000 per year, depending upon their employer and industry. Government and media careerists tend to earn the most money, while those working in the healthcare and social services sectors tend to earn a little less. Freelancers can charge anywhere from $15 to $40 per hour for their services. This depends on the kind of contracts freelancers are able to negotiate and on the language or languages in which they work.

Urdu, for example, is generally worth more per hour than Spanish, but the market for Urdu linguists is not very large.

Teachers can earn anywhere from $35,000 per year to $85,000 per year depending upon the school district and other factors like seniority and advanced degrees.

A few things to keep in mind. Translation and interpretation can be routine and monotonous or they can be wonderfully exciting. A job translating documents for a business may come with regular hours and a steady paycheck but may not be the most interesting opportunity. On the other hand, adventurous people who combine some translation and interpretation with teaching TESOL and traveling, can lead fascinating lives filled with a constant flow of new experiences. They may also live paycheck-to-paycheck, which is not ideal, but they will have fun doing it. Only you can determine what you value the most – adventure or predictability.

This is something you should be thinking about. Many careerists look at job opportunities through a lens of specific benefits like salary, potential for bonuses, paid vacation time, health insurance and the like. They also assess how much they will enjoy a particular job and what it will bring to their life experience. Given the nature of your career, however, you owe it to yourself to take the long view and plan to take advantage of the many opportunities a career in languages can afford you. See the world while you are young and unattached. The day will come when you will want things like a family and a mortgage, so have as many adventures as you can before you get the urge to settle down.

OPPORTUNITIES

YOU COULD NOT HAVE CHOSEN A BETTER time to enter this profession. Demand is expected to grow rapidly in the coming years. You have undoubtedly heard that the world is becoming a smaller place, that globalization and the internet have combined to make almost everybody next door neighbors. We can video chat with anybody anywhere, conduct business all over the world with ease, and cater to markets that were almost inaccessible only a few years ago. Regular people routinely take their vacations in places that used to be the province of only the most seasoned adventurers. All of these factors and more have boosted demand for foreign language expertise to new heights. Opportunities abound and there will be more as time goes by. Assuming you are a native English speaker, you already have an advantage in being fluent in the world's most spoken language, the target language with the greatest demand for translation and interpretation.

You can also make yourself more competitive by earning additional credentials and polishing up your résumé. A TESOL certificate will open many doors and allow you to pick and choose your next adventures. Service in the military or the Peace Corps will earn extra credibility. Earning an advanced degree will move your résumé to the top of the stack, especially if you major in something complementary to your main focus on languages. Learning additional languages will always be beneficial to your career, particularly if your resulting skills give you mastery over a particular industry or geographical area. Linguists working in Arabic often also learn French, for example, because much of the Arabic speaking world also uses French. A linguist with skills in French and Portuguese – in addition to English – could carve out a very nice career in Sub-Saharan Africa. Both kinds of Chinese – Cantonese and Mandarin – would offer almost innumerable opportunities dealing with the world's second largest economy.

Languages may not be at the center of your career forever. A career as a linguist could lead to a second career in a number of fields, including travel, international commerce, or diplomacy. The world is filled with careerists who earn MBA degrees in the hope of building a career in international business, for example. Many careerists take this route because they like to travel or because international business sounds more exciting than domestic business. You would be amazed, however, at how many globetrotting business people do not speak a second language. Your skills will give you a huge advantage over them.

GETTING STARTED

WHEN THE TIME COMES TO GET your first real job you will need to step out with confidence. Get your personal marketing materials in order. A résumé is a necessity. Take the time to write a good one. There are many books and software applications that can help you to put together a top-notch résumé. If you want additional help your college outplacement office should be able to offer some assistance. You can also hire a professional résumé writer. Do not skimp on this process. Writing a traditionally formatted résumé will help you to organize your experience and expertise, and will help you to focus on what you want. A résumé will also make it much easier to fill out online applications because you can cut and paste information from your résumé into online forms. You may also need a traditionally formatted résumé to give to a potential employer in paper or digital form.

More people get jobs through personal connections than by any other means. Remember this as you meet people during your college years. Professors, employers, internship supervisors, and anybody else who may be in a position to offer you a job, referral or recommendation are all worth keeping in touch with.

Maintaining these relationships will pay off when the time comes to look for your first full-time job. Send your résumé to all of the people on your list and see what kind of response you get. You may be surprised. If something strikes your fancy, take it.

This is your first real job. Do not get hung up on the details. It does not have to be your dream job. In fact, at this stage you probably will not really know what your dream job is. That is a question that cannot be answered until you have spent a few years in the profession. That is the only way to triangulate on what you really want to do. This process will come with a few disappointments, but it will also come with quite a few exciting discoveries. The first step in the process is to get started. Good luck!

ASSOCIATIONS, PERIODICALS, WEBSITES

■ **Alta Language Training**
www.altalang.com

■ **American Council on the Teaching of Foreign Languages**
www.actfl.org

■ **American Literary Translators Association**
www.literarytranslators.org

■ **American Translators Association**
www.atanet.org

■ **American University**
www.american.edu

■ **Association of Language Companies**
www.alcus.org

■ **British Broadcasting Corporation**
www.bbc.co.uk

■ **California State University, Los Angeles**
www.calstatela.edu

■ **Department of State**
www.state.gov

■ **Florida International University**
www.fiu.edu

■ **France 24**
www.france24.com

■ **Go Abroad**
www.goabroad.com

■ **Hunter College**
www.hunter.cuny.edu

■ **International Association for Translation and Intercultural Studies**
www.iatis.org

■ **International Association of Conference Interpreters**
www.aiic.net

■ **International Association of Professional Translators and Interpreters**
www.iapti.org

■ **International Center for Language Studies**
www.icls.com

■ **International Federation of Translators**
www.fit-ift.org

- **James Madison University**
www.jmu.edu

- **Language Scientific**
www.languagescientific.com

- **Marygrove College**
www.marygrove.edu

- **National Council on Interpreting in Health Care**
www.ncihc.org

- **Omniglot**
www.omniglot.com

- **Rosetta Stone**
www.rosettastone.com

- **San Diego State University**
www.sdsu.edu

- **TESOL International Association**
www.tesol.org

- **Transitions Abroad**
www.transitionsabroad.com

- **Translator Training**
www.translator-training.com

- **Translators Without Borders**
www.translatorswithoutborders.org

- **United States Air Force**
www.airforce.com

- **United States Army**
www.goarmy.com

■ **United States Marine Corps**
www.marines.com

■ **United States Navy**
www.navy.com

■ **University of Arkansas**
www.uark.edu

■ **University of Charleston**
www.ucwv.edu

■ **University of Illinois**
www.illinois.edu

■ **University of Maryland**
www.umd.edu

■ **University of Nebraska at Kearney**
www.unk.edu

■ **University of Pittsburgh**
www.pitt.edu

■ **University of Wisconsin Milwaukee**
www.uwm.edu

Made in the USA
Coppell, TX
22 November 2019